# A Day in the Life: Grassland Animals

# Hyena

Louise Spilsbury

Raintree

**www.raintreepublishers.co.uk**
Visit our website to find out more information about Raintree books.

**To order:**
☎ Phone 0845 6044371
🖶 Fax +44 (0) 1865 312263
📧 Email myorders@raintreepublishers.co.uk

Customers from outside the UK please telephone +44 1865 312262

Raintree is an imprint of Capstone Global Library Limited, a company incorporated in England and Wales having its registered office at 7 Pilgrim Street, London, EC4V 6LB – Registered company number: 6695582

Text © Capstone Global Library Limited 2011
First published in hardback in 2011
Paperback edition first published in 2012
The moral rights of the proprietor have been asserted.

Edited by Dan Nunn, Rebecca Rissman, Catherine Veitch and Nancy Dickmann
Designed by Philippa Jenkins
Picture research by Mica Brancic
Originated by Capstone Global Library
Printed and bound in China by South China Printing Company Ltd

ISBN 978 1 406 21898 5 (hardback)
15 14 13 12 11
10 9 8 7 6 5 4 3 2 1

ISBN 978 1 406 21902 9 (paperback)
16 15 14 13 12
10 9 8 7 6 5 4 3 2 1

**British Library Cataloguing in Publication Data**
Spilsbury, Louise.
Hyena. -- (A day in the life. Grassland animals)
599.7'43-dc22
A full catalogue record for this book is available from the British Library.

**Acknowledgements**
We would like to thank the following for permission to reproduce photographs: Alamy pp. 5, 23 clan (© Ann and Steve Toon); Corbis pp. 7, 23 male (fstop/© Sean Russell); FLPA pp. 13, 15, 20, 23 den (Minden Pictures/Suzi Eszterhas); iStockphoto p. 23 wildebeest (Robert Hardholt); Nature Picture Library pp. 14 (© Martin Dohrn), 16 (© Hermann Brehm); Photolibrary p. 21 (Oxford Scientific (OSF)/Richard Packwood); Photoshot pp. 10, 11, 23 territory (© NHPA/Nigel J Dennis), 18 (© NHPA/Martin Harvey); Shutterstock pp. 4 (© erllre74), 6, 22 (© EcoPrint), 9, 23 grassland (© Jay Bo), 12 (p.schwarz ), 17 (Ecoimages), 19, 23 female (© Steffen Foerster Photography).

Cover photograph of a portrait of a spotted hyena, Etosha National Park, Namibia, reproduced with permission of Shutterstock (© EcoPrint). Back cover photographs of (left) a hyena showing its teeth reproduced with permission of FLPA (Minden Pictures/Suzi Eszterhas) and (right) hyenas in a den reproduced with permission of FLPA (Minden Pictures/ Suzi Eszterhas).

We would like to thank Michael Bright for his invaluable help in the preparation of this book.

The author would like to dedicate this book to her nephew and niece, Ben and Amelie: "I wrote these books for animal lovers like you. I hope you enjoy them." Aunty Louise.

# Contents

Some words are in bold, **like this**. You can find out what they mean by looking in the glossary.

# What is a hyena?

A hyena is an animal that looks a bit like a dog.

A hyena has a big head and strong jaws.

Hyenas live in groups of between 5 to 80 animals, called **clans**.

A clan of hyenas is so fierce that even lions do not hunt them!

# What do spotted hyenas look like?

Spotted hyenas have short, sand-coloured fur with brown spots.

They have a long neck, a sloping back, and a short bushy tail.

female

male

**Male** and **female** spotted hyenas look the same, but females are a tiny bit bigger.

Female hyenas are the leaders of the **clan**!

# Where do spotted hyenas live?

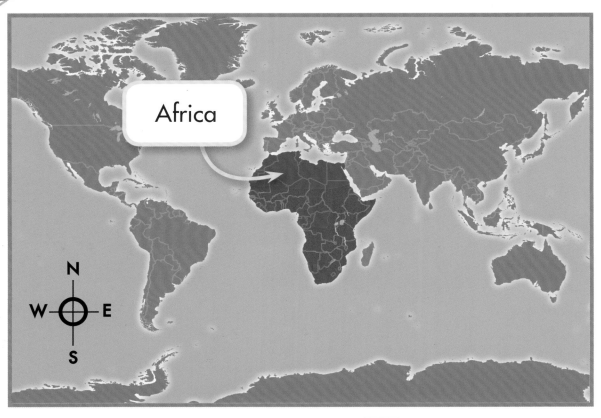

Africa

key: ■ = where hyenas live

Spotted hyenas live in many parts of Africa.

Most spotted hyenas live in **grasslands**.

In these grasslands the land is covered in grasses and a few trees.

It is mostly hot and dry here, but some months it rains a lot.

# What do hyenas do at night?

Hyenas get up at night to hunt for food.

Hyenas in a **clan** stay in an area called their **territory** at night.

At night they mark their territory with scratches and smells.

These marks warn hyenas from other clans to keep away.

# What do hyenas eat?

wildebeest

Hyenas eat big animals like zebra and **wildebeest**.

They also eat small animals or dead animals caught by wild dogs or lions.

Hyenas have strong teeth that can bite through meat and bones.

Hyenas eat so many bones that their droppings are often white!

# How do hyenas hunt?

Hyenas use hearing, smell, and sight to find food at night.

They run fast and can chase animals without getting tired.

Hyenas usually hunt together.

They chase a weak, old, or sick animal until they catch it.

# Do hyenas laugh?

Hyenas laugh or giggle when they are scared or excited.

Hyenas make other sounds too, like growling and yelling.

At night hyenas make sounds to tell each other things in the dark.

They whoop, howl, and scream when they are hunting.

# What are spotted hyena babies like?

Baby hyenas are dark brown.

They drink milk from their mother during the day, and rest at night.

At about one year old, cubs learn to hunt with their mother at night.

Then they can go hunting with the rest of the **clan**.

# What do hyenas do during the day?

den

During the day, a hyena goes back to its **den** to rest and sleep.

A den is a big hole in the ground or in rock.

If it is very hot, hyenas may find pools of water to sit in.

Mother hyenas also feed their babies and watch them play.

# Hyena body map

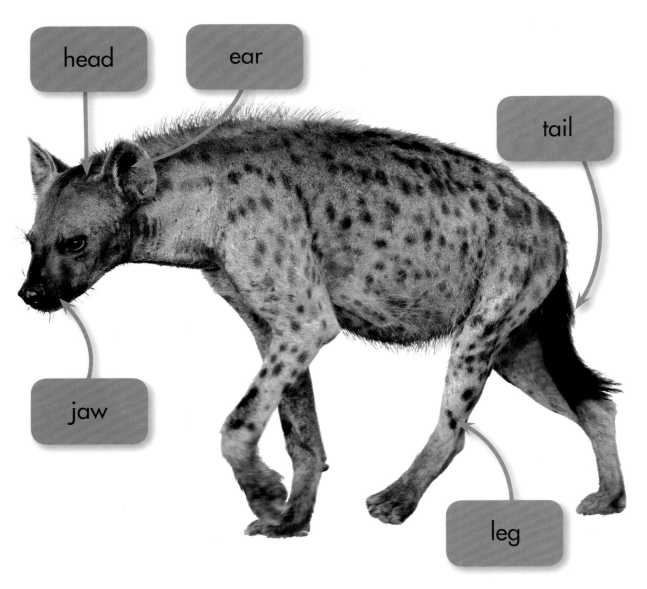

head

ear

tail

jaw

leg

# Glossary

 **clan** group of hyenas

 **den** hole in the ground or in rock where a wild animal lives

 **female** animal that can become a mother when it is grown up

 **grassland** land where mostly grasses grow

 **male** animal that can become a father when it is grown up

 **territory** area of land belonging to an animal or group of animals

 **wildebeest** large African antelope with a long head, a beard and mane, and a sloping back

# Find out more

## Books

*Grassland Food Chains*, Richard and Louise Spilsbury
   (Heinemann Library, 2004)
*Hyenas (Scary Creatures)*, John Malam (Book House, 2009)

## Websites

http://animals.nationalgeographic.com/animals/mammals/
   hyena.html
http://www.sandiegozoo.org/animalbytes/t-striped_hyena.html

# Index